ANOTHER DAY
IN CUBICLE
PARADISE

Other DILBERT books from Boxtree

When Did Ignorance Become a Point of View
ISBN: 0-7522-2412-3

Excuse Me While I Wag
ISBN: 0-7522-2399-2

Dilbert-A Treasury of Sunday Strips: Version 00
ISBN: 0-7522-7232-2

Random Acts of Management
ISBN: 0-7522-7174-1

Dilbert Gives You the Business
ISBN: 0-7522-2394-1

Don't Step in the Leadership
ISBN: 0-7522-2389-5

Journey to Cubeville
ISBN: 0-7522-2384-4

I'm Not Anti-Business, I'm Anti-Idiot
ISBN: 0-7522-2379-8

Seven Years of Highly Defective People
ISBN: 0-7522-2407-7

Casual Day Has Gone Too Far
ISBN: 0-7522-1119-6

Fugitive from the Cubicle Police
ISBN: 0-7522-2431-X

Still Pumped from Using the Mouse
ISBN: 0-7522-2265-1

It's Obvious You Won't Survive by Your Wits Alone
ISBN: 0-7522-0201-4

Bring Me the Head of Willy the Mailboy!
ISBN: 0-7522-0136-0

Shave the Whales
ISBN: 0-7522-0849-7

Always Postpone Meetings with Time-Wasting Morons
ISBN: 0-7522-0854-3

ANOTHER DAY
IN CUBICLE
PARADISE

A DILBERT™ BOOK
BY SCOTT ADAMS

BOXTREE

First published 2002 by Andrews McMeel Publishing, an Andrews McMeel Universal company,
4520 Main Street, Kansas City, Missouri 64111

First published in Great Britain 2002 by Boxtree
an imprint of Pan Macmillan Ltd
Pan Macmillan, 20 New Wharf Road, London N1 9RR
Basingstoke and Oxford
Associated companies throughout the world
www.panmacmillan.com

ISBN 0 7522 2486 7

9 8 7 6 5 4 3 2

A CIP catalogue record for this book is available from the British Library

Printed by the Bath Press Ltd, Bath

For the best negative shopper ever

Introduction

Someone wise once said (Okay, it was me, about a minute ago), "Never sit for eight hours a day in a fabric-covered box that someone else paid for." And then it hit me. I finally figured out what's wrong with the whole cubicle concept: Communism.

That's right; cubicles are a form of communism. Think about it. You don't own your cubicle — the "state" does. Well, technically your stockholders own the cubicle, not the state, but it's the same problem. Because the people who pay for your cubicle don't have to sit in it, there's no incentive for cubicles to be all that they can be. It's no wonder they're bleak and dingy.

Maybe it's time to lift the yoke of communism from the oppressed cubicle masses. I say every employee should own his or her cubicle and take it along to every new assignment. The cubicle of the future would be modular so you can easily relocate it and customize it to taste. Sure, this new system would introduce some annoying eccentricities into the system. Every person would have a different idea of what the perfect cubicle should be. Your neighbors might have low-rider cubicles and Barbie-themed cubicles and maybe the clothing-optional, disco cubicles. But that's a small price to pay for the freedom to customize your own workspace.

I would decorate my cubicle like the inside of a womb, except with better electronic gadgetry. I wouldn't need a chair. I'd just curl up in a fetal position near my keyboard. When you're in a womb, it feels as if your life is full of possibilities and all of them are ahead of you. You feel warm and fed and loved. And I think I'd put censors at the doorway (the design of which I shall not describe), so that when I left my womb-cube a motherly voice would scream as if giving birth. It might annoy my cubicle neighbors, but we can take that up at the next meeting of the Cube-Owners Association.

Speaking of wonderful things, there's still time to join Dogbert's New Ruling Class (DNRC) and be by his side when he conquers the world and makes everyone else our domestic servants. To be a member all you need to do is sign up for the free *Dilbert Newsletter* that is published approximately whenever I feel like it — about five times a year if you're lucky.

To subscribe or unsubscribe, go to www.dilbert.com. If you have problems with the automated subscription method, write to newsletter@unitedmedia.com.

S. Adams

Scott Adams

OUR CEO SAYS WE ARE POISED FOR HUGE GROWTH IN EARNINGS.

IN AN UNRELATED MOVE, HE ANNOUNCED THAT HE WILL LEAVE THE COMPANY BEFORE ANY OF HIS STOCK OPTIONS VEST.

THE POOR GUY WILL MISS ALL OF OUR GROWTH.

IS THAT WORK? I CAN'T SEE WHAT'S ON THE SCREEN.

IF HE SEES ME I'LL PRETEND I'M IN MID-STRIDE, JUST PASSING BY.

THE SMALL FONT IS WORKING.

MUSCLES CRAMPING.

GOOD.

SMILE, ALICE. IT WON'T HURT.

GAAAK!!

I FOUND OUT I CAN KILL PEOPLE BY LOOKING AT THEM.

I WONDERED WHY YOU WERE SMIL-ING.

THE KEY TO HAPPINESS IS SELF-DELUSION.

DON'T THINK OF YOURSELF AS AN ORGANIC PAIN COLLECTOR RACING TOWARD OBLIVION.

I'VE NEVER HAD THAT THOUGHT... UNTIL NOW.

DON'T BLAME ME; I SAID DON'T.

I'M A NATURE LOVER. WHEN I FISH, I ONLY DO CATCH-AND-RELEASE.

IN OTHER WORDS, YOU TORTURE FISH FOR FUN.

I WONDER WHY EVERYTHING I DO SOUNDS BAD WHEN IT'S PUT IN OTHER WORDS.

GOOD NEWS: THE DEADLINE GOT PUSHED BACK A WEEK.

GOOD NEWS?! I'VE BEEN WORKING FOR FORTY HOURS STRAIGHT TO FINISH ON TIME!

I JUST REALIZED I DON'T KNOW THE DIFFERENCE BETWEEN GOOD NEWS AND BAD NEWS.

WHAT IS THIS STRANGE AND BEAUTIFUL FEELING INSIDE OF ME?!

WAVES OF ECSTASY ARE PULSING THROUGH MY SOUL.

THIS IS WHY I ONLY GIVE POSITIVE REINFORCEMENT ONCE A YEAR.

I'M ALL TINGLY!

I EXPERIENCED SOMETHING CALLED POSITIVE REINFORCEMENT TODAY.

I'M ADDICTED TO IT NOW... BUT IT'S WEARING OFF... MUST GET MORE...

SAY SOMETHING NICE ABOUT ME!

FOR A CRAZY WOMAN YOU DON'T DROOL MUCH.

I'M ADDICTED TO POSITIVE REINFORCEMENT.

I NEED SOME DELIVERABLES SO I CAN BE PRAISED AGAIN.

RESULTS

MANAGEMENT TRAINING

YOU TWIST THE EARS TO UNLOCK THE SKULL.

FIND THE MORAL COMPASS AND DEACTIVATE IT.

THE RESULT IS SOMETHING CALLED LEADERSHIP.

YOU'RE WORKING WEEKENDS!

MANAGEMENT TRAINING

TIM WILL DEMONSTRATE THE MANAGEMENT CLOAK OF INVISIBILITY.

I ADMIT IT DOESN'T SEEM VERY SPECIAL WHEN YOU KNOW HOW IT'S DONE.

HOW DO YOU LIKE BEING A MANAGER, ALICE?

DO ME A BIG FAVOR; SNEAK INTO MY HOUSE TONIGHT AND SMOTHER ME WITH A PILLOW.

I THINK SHE WAS KIDDING.

I'LL SEE IF SHE PUTS UP A STRUGGLE.

20

THE MASTER OF DEL-EGATION HEARS THE FOOTSTEPS OF HIS PREY.

HI

GAAA!!

CALL THIS VENDOR AND TELL HIM I WANT THE THIRD THING HE TOLD ME ABOUT.

OKAY. THAT WILL SAVE TWO MINUTES OF YOUR VALUABLE TIME.

WHEN THE VENDOR ASKS ME DOZENS OF QUESTIONS SHOULD I JUST GUESS AT THE ANSWERS?

OR WOULD YOU PREFER TO SPEND AN HOUR GIVING ME ENOUGH BACKGROUND SO YOU CAN AVOID A TWO-MINUTE CALL?

YOU KNOW WHAT'S FUNNY? THIS CONVERSATION LASTED A MINUTE... AND THERE ARE TWO OF US.

ARE YOU DONE?

I THINK YOU WROTE DOWN YOUR OWN PHONE NUMBER.

24

Panel 1: I'M PROMOTING YOU TO PRESIDENT OF OUR DOT-COM SUBSIDIARY.

Panel 2: YOUR JOB IS TO FIRE EVERYONE.

Panel 3: WOULD I GET A RAISE? / HOW DOES A BILLION SHARES OF STOCK SOUND?

Panel 4: DILBERT: DOT-COM CEO

WE HAVE NO PROFIT NOW AND WE NEVER WILL. YOU'RE ALL LAID OFF.

Panel 5: DOES ANYONE KNOW WHAT LAID OFF MEANS? / IT MUST BE A COMPLIMENT.

Panel 6: YOU'RE PRETTY LAID OFF YOUR-SELF, DUDE. / WANT A HIT OF THIS?

Panel 7: DOGBERT'S TECH SUPPORT

YOUR MOUSEPAD IS INCOMPATIBLE WITH YOUR OPER-ATING SYSTEM.

Panel 8: TRY REBOOTING THE MOUSEPAD. IF THAT DOESN'T WORK, I'LL CALL YOU BACK.

Panel 9: HOW WILL YOU KNOW? / I'LL WATCH YOU THROUGH YOUR MONITOR.

26

WE NEED TO REDUCE STAFF BY TWENTY.

HERE'S A LIST OF THE PEOPLE YOU'VE A-L-M-O-S-T WORKED TO DEATH.

I HAVE ANOTHER PROJECT FOR YOU ...UH...TED.

AACK!

I HOPE SHE'S HOME.

BEEP BOOP BEEP

IF YOU'D LIKE TO TAKE ME TO PARIS, PRESS ONE. IF YOU ARE INVITING ME TO A LOUSY MOVIE, PRESS TWO.

I'VE GOT A BAD FEELING ABOUT THIS.

BEEP

I LIKE TAKE-CHARGE MEN WHO JUST SAY, "C'MON, WE'RE GOING SOMEPLACE."

C'MON, WE'RE GOING TO THE BOWLING ALLEY!

THAT'S THE DUMBEST IDEA I'VE EVER HEARD.

I THINK I SEE HOW THIS WORKS.

YOU DON'T GIVE YOUR OPINION ON ANYTHING. ARE YOU SPINELESS?

MAYBE YOU CREATE AN ENVIRONMENT IN WHICH GIVING AN OPINION IS AN INVITATION TO UNNECESSARY PAIN.

GREAT! YOU'RE MAKING ME CRY IN PUBLIC!!

WE CAN'T SHOW THESE NUMBERS TO OUR VP. THEY MAKE US LOOK LIKE LOSERS.

FIND SOMETHING WE'RE DOING WELL AND GIVE HIM THOSE NUMBERS INSTEAD.

WOW! OUR INTERNAL SUBTERFUGE IS UP EIGHTY PERCENT!

WE TRY TO RETAIN OUR BEST EMPLOYEES BY GIVING THEM "GOLDEN HANDCUFFS."

THE REST OF YOU WILL EXPERIENCE OUR OTHER PROGRAM, THE ONE I CALL "PRICKLY PANTIES."

THEN HE GAVE ME A HUGE BOWL OF CANDY.

HEY, THEY CUT OUR DENTAL PLAN AGAIN!

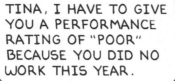

TINA, I HAVE TO GIVE YOU A PERFORMANCE RATING OF "POOR" BECAUSE YOU DID NO WORK THIS YEAR.

NO WORK?

I WROTE HUNDREDS OF TECHNICAL DOCUMENTS THIS YEAR!

I WORKED SEVENTY HOURS A WEEK!

I E-MAILED EVERY ONE OF THE DOCUMENTS TO YOU...

...WITH INSTRUCTIONS TO FORWARD THEM WITH YOUR APPROVAL TO THE END USERS.

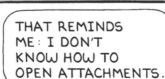

THAT REMINDS ME: I DON'T KNOW HOW TO OPEN ATTACHMENTS.

WHY DIDN'T YOU TELL ME YOU NEVER GOT MY DOCUMENTS?

WHO ARE YOU?

3/25/01 © 2001 United Feature Syndicate, Inc.

29

32

WHY AREN'T YOU SIGNED UP FOR THE 401K?

I'D NEVER BE ABLE TO RUN THAT FAR.

I DID A 10K WHEELCHAIR RACE ONCE. THE GUY WHO PUSHED ME STILL HAS WHIP MARKS.

WHICH ASSIGNMENT IS THE HIGHEST PRIORITY?

IS IT THE TOTALLY WORTHLESS ONE OR THE OTHER TOTALLY WORTHLESS ONE?

I HOPE I'M EMPOWERED TO MAKE THAT DECISION.

HOPE IS A DOUBLE-EDGED SWORD.

THEY CAN MAKE ME WORK IN A LITTLE BOX, BUT THEY CAN'T CRUSH MY SPIRIT.

OUR ISO 9000 COORDINATOR DIED OF BOREDOM. YOU'LL HAVE TO DO HIS JOB PLUS YOURS.

AND ONE OF THE QUALITY ASSURANCE GUYS IS LOOKING PALE...

WOW! I'VE BEEN SELECTED FOR THE "WHO'S INCREDIBLE" LIST!

FOR SEVENTY-FIVE DOLLARS I CAN BUY A LEATHER-BOUND BOOK WITH MY NAME IN IT!

HA! AND PEOPLE SAID I WAS TOO GULLIBLE TO BE A SUCCESS!

"DEAR OCCUPANT"

I'M BRINGING MY COPY OF "WHO'S INCREDIBLE" TO MY HIGH SCHOOL REUNION.

IF ANYONE ASKS HOW I'M DOING, I'LL CASUALLY OPEN THE BOOK AND POINT TO MY NAME.

I GOT RICH SELLING A BOOK CALLED "WHO'S INCREDIBLE" TO GULLIBLE PEOPLE.

HIGH SCHOOL REUNION

I STARTED WITH NOTHING. NOW I HAVE MY OWN CUBICLE.

SAY, NOW THAT WE'RE BOTH ADULTS, WOULD YOU LIKE TO... YOU KNOW?

YES.

I'VE GOT TO BE MORE SPECIFIC.

DID YOU CALL ME HERE TO PUNISH ME?

NO, NO, ASOK. I WANT YOU TO MANAGE OUR ANNUAL BUSINESS PLAN PROCESS.

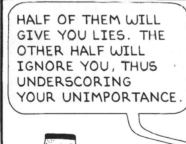

HOW DO I DO THAT?

FIRST, YOU BEG YOUR CO-WORKERS FOR INFORMATION ABOUT THEIR BUDGET NEEDS.

HALF OF THEM WILL GIVE YOU LIES. THE OTHER HALF WILL IGNORE YOU, THUS UNDERSCORING YOUR UNIMPORTANCE.

THEN YOU'LL COMBINE THE LIES AND GUESSES INTO A WORTHLESS BALL OF DATA FOR SENIOR MANAGEMENT.

THEN OUR CEO WILL MAKE BUDGET DECISIONS BASED ON MAGAZINE ARTICLES.

HOW BAD WAS THE PUNISHMENT?

WORSE THAN I EXPECTED.

4/8/01 © 2001 United Feature Syndicate, Inc.

35

WE'VE DISCOVERED OIL IN THE ELBONIAN WILD-LIFE PRESERVE.

DON'T WORRY ABOUT THE ENDANGERED SPECIES. OUR DRILLING WILL HAVE NO IMPACT.

OOPS

I'M SAD TO REPORT THAT OUR OIL DRILLING HAS CAUSED THE EXTINCTION OF THE ELBONIAN UNICORN.

SAVE A SAMPLE OF THE ANIMAL'S DNA SO WE CAN CLONE A NEW ONE.

DON'T FINISH THAT.

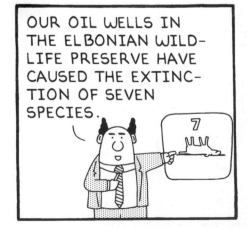

OUR OIL WELLS IN THE ELBONIAN WILD-LIFE PRESERVE HAVE CAUSED THE EXTINC-TION OF SEVEN SPECIES.

LUCKILY, THEY WERE USELESS SPECIES WHO DID NOTHING BUT EAT AND GRUNT.

MM...
MM...
MM...

NOW FOR THE WEEKLY WALLY REPORT.

WALLY STRUGGLED TO MAINTAIN HIS MORALE DESPITE THE NINETY PERCENT DROP IN HIS STOCK OPTIONS.

THEN HE REMEMBERED THAT SOMEONE LOST MUCH, MUCH, MUCH MORE THAN HE DID.

THE KEY TO SUCCESS IS TO REMAIN OPTIMISTIC EVEN WHEN YOU FAIL.

WHAT'S THE POINT OF SUCCEEDING IF FAILING FEELS GOOD TOO?

I'LL READ ANOTHER PAGE OF THAT MAGAZINE ARTICLE TOMORROW AND GET BACK TO YOU.

MAYBE I CAN STAVE OFF THE BOREDOM BY IMAGINING MY CO-WORKERS NAKED.

AAAGH! NO-O-O-O!!!

NO MORE DONUTS FOR YOU.

HEY, DON'T EVEN KID ABOUT THAT.

OUR INDUSTRY IS IN A SLUMP. WE NEED TO MAKE CHANGES.

OUR CURRENT MANAGEMENT STYLE COULD BE DESCRIBED AS PATERNAL.

OUR NEW MANAGEMENT STYLE DOESN'T HAVE A NAME YET.

OOH OOH! I HAVE A SUGGESTION.

THE NEW MANAGEMENT STYLE COULD BE CALLED "WE HATE OUR EMPLOYEES."

NOT BAD.

I NEED A VOLUNTEER TO HELP WITH OUR "BACK TO THE NINETIES" KICK-OFF.

HOW IS THIS LIKE THE NINETIES?

STOP WIGGLING!

MY NEXT GENERATION INTERNET PROJECT IS RIGHT ON SCHEDULE.

IT'LL BE DONE SOMETIME IN THE NEXT GENERATION.

IF YOU KNOW ANY CUTE SINGLE WOMEN WITH LOW STANDARDS, IT WOULD REALLY HELP.

A HAPPY DILBERT PREPARES TO GO HOME AFTER A LONG DAY IN THE CUBICLE.

TOO LATE! THE SIX O'CLOCK HORROR IS UPON HIM!

GAAA!!!

IN YOUR WORKSPACE NO ONE CAN HEAR YOU SCREAM.

WHAT WAS THAT?

JUST KEEP WALKING.

A NIGERIAN BANKER NEEDS MY HELP GETTING THIRTY MILLION DOLLARS OUT OF HIS COUNTRY!

ALL I NEED TO DO IS GIVE HIM MY BANK INFORMATION BY E-MAIL AND I'LL GET A TEN PERCENT COMMISSION!

DEAR GUSTAVA,

MY BANK IS A TUBE SOCK THAT FELL BEHIND THE DRYER.

SOMEONE THREW A COMPUTER OFF THE ROOF AND KILLED OUR BIGGEST CUSTOMER.

WE PLAN TO REPLACE HIM WITH A LOOK-ALIKE WHO WILL CONTINUE BUYING FROM US.

HEY, THAT'S WILLY FROM THE CLUB OF PEOPLE WHO LOOK EXACTLY LIKE ME.

YOU'LL IMPERSONATE OUR DEAD CUSTOMER AND MAKE LARGE PURCHASES FROM US.

I'VE NEVER DONE ANY-THING LIKE THIS BEFORE.

IT'S CALLED "WORK."

AM I DOING IT RIGHT?

WALLY'S IN JAIL FOR IMPERSONATING A DEAD PERSON.

HE'LL HAVE TO USE ALL OF HIS STREET SMARTS TO SURVIVE.

I'LL NEED SOME TEMPORARY TATTOOS. WHICH WAY IS THE GIFT SHOP?

WALLY'S IN JAIL. CAN YOU HELP GET HIM OUT?

TELL HIM TO TRY THE DOOR. THE GUARDS ONLY PRETEND TO LOCK THEM.

BUT I'D HAVE TO SAY IT WAS THE LIFERS WHO WERE THE MOST EMBAR- RASSED.

WALLY, NOW THAT YOU HAVE A CRIMINAL RECORD, I CAN'T LET YOU WORK ON ANY- THING IMPORTANT.

I DON'T HAVE A CRIMINAL RECORD. I GAVE THE POLICE A FAKE NAME.

YOU MIGHT NOTICE A CHANGE IN THE QUALITY OF YOUR ASSIGNMENTS.

THERE AREN'T ENOUGH FRIENDLY PEOPLE TO FILL OUR CALL CENTER JOBS.

ALL WE CAN FIND ARE ANGRY PEOPLE WHO REFUSE TO PUT THEIR TELEPHONE HEADSET MICROPHONES NEAR THEIR MOUTHS.

NO, I'M SURE THE PROBLEM IS ON YOUR END.

CAROL, YOUR OVERALL PERFORMANCE RATING IS "GOOD."

AAAG! GOOD IS BAD! WHAT DID I DO TO DESERVE THIS HUMILIATION.

WELL, YOU GAVE ME SIX HUNDRED PHONE MESSAGES THAT SAID, "IT MIGHT HAVE BEEN BOB."

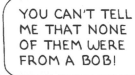

YOU CAN'T TELL ME THAT NONE OF THEM WERE FROM A BOB!

YOU ARRANGED FOR ALL OF MY FLIGHTS TO HAVE CONNECTIONS IN WAR ZONES.

EXCUSE ME FOR TRYING TO SAVE THE COMPANY SOME MONEY.

YOU HELD A PRESS CONFERENCE TO ANNOUNCE THAT I WAS THE PARKSIDE STRANGLER.

AND HE REFUSES TO TAKE ANY RESPONSIBILITY FOR GIVING ME VAGUE OBJECTIVES.

CAROL, SCREEN MY CALLS AND DON'T LET ANY SALES-PEOPLE THROUGH.

HELLO, I'M A HUGE CUSTOMER OR PERHAPS A CHILDHOOD FRIEND OF YOUR BOSS.

GIVE ME SOME FLIRTING AND YOU'RE IN.

IS IT HOT IN HERE OR IS IT JUST YOU?

CAROL, WHY DO YOU KEEP PUTTING SALES PEOPLE THROUGH TO ME?

I'M TAKING BRIBES TO SUPPLEMENT MY INCOME. IT'S A NATURAL EXTENSION OF EMPOWERMENT.

I SENSE SOME MICROMANAGEMENT BREWING.

CAROL, YOU CAN'T KEEP ACCEPTING BRIBES FROM SALES PEOPLE WHO WANT ACCESS TO ME.

BAD!

DIDN'T A VENDOR RECENTLY TAKE YOU ON A GOLF TRIP TO VEGAS?

THAT IS SO-O-O DIFFER-ENT!

LET'S COMPARE PRICE SHEETS.

I'M MEETING A VENDOR FOR DRINKS TONIGHT. HE SAYS IT'S THE ONLY TIME HE HAS TO ANSWER MY QUESTIONS.

IF THAT WORKS, PLEASE LET US KNOW.

WHAT DO YOU MEAN "WORKS"? AND WHO IS "US"?

IT'S ALREADY WORKING!

A VENDOR INVITED ME FOR DRINKS. IT'S THE ONLY TIME HE HAS TO TALK ABOUT HIS PRODUCT.

HE'S USING THE OLD BAIT-LUBE-AND-SWITCH TRICK. THAT'S HOW I GOT MY FIRST AND THIRD WIVES.

I DON'T UNDER-STAND.

THAT'S WHY IT WORKS.

THIS IS STRICTLY BUSINESS, RIGHT? WE'RE GOING TO TALK ABOUT YOUR COMPANY'S PRODUCT.

I'LL BET I CAN CHUG MORE CHARDONNAY THAN YOU CAN.

YOU'RE A HANSHUM MAN AND SO ISH YOUR TWIN BRUVER.

BURP

I'M DATING AN UNATTRACTIVE MAN. WHAT SHOULD I DO?

EVERY MAN IS UGLY UNTIL A WOMAN FIXES HIM UP. THINK OF IT AS A PROJECT.

NEXT, LOSE THE COMB-OVER, OR AT LEAST STAY OUT OF THE WIND.

HOW'D YOU KNOW ABOUT THE COMB-OVER?

THE BOYFRIEND PROJECT

I'M PUTTING YOU IN TURTLENECKS AND JEANS.

YOU DON'T LIKE TO FISH ANYMORE. NOW YOU'RE TRAINING FOR MARATHONS.

WHAA! WHAA!

YOU CAN ONLY CRY AT MOVIES.

THE BOYFRIEND PROJECT

YOU'RE MAKING GOOD PROGRESS.

Before

I'M READY TO BE SEEN WITH YOU IN PUBLIC. BUT DON'T DO ANY TALKING.

...AND THAT'S WHY I THINK THERE SHOULD BE A NOBEL PRIZE FOR WRESTLING.

I SAID...

...AND THAT'S WHY I RECOMMEND USING THIS VENDOR.

$PXH!.COM

WHY DON'T WE USE OUR INTERNAL DEVELOPERS?

LET ME EXPLAIN HOW THIS WILL PLAY OUT.

STEP ONE: WE SELECT AN OUTSIDE VENDOR BECAUSE OUR INTERNAL DEVELOPERS ARE CLUELESS WEASELS.

STEP TWO: WE SIGN A CONTRACT AND BEGIN WORK.

STEP THREE: OUR INTERNAL WEASELS COMPLAIN TO OUR VP AND SHE ORDERS US TO USE THEM.

STEP FOUR: THE OUTSIDE VENDOR SUES US WHILE OUR WEASELS GRUNT OUT STEAMING MOUNDS OF WORTHLESS CODE.

DO I PLAN TOO MUCH?

IS THIS THE CONVERSATION WE PRACTICED YESTERDAY?

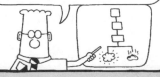

DILBERT, I'D LIKE YOU TO MEET INCREDULOUS ED.

NO MATTER WHAT QUESTION YOU ASK HIM, HE'LL REACT AS IF YOU'RE INVENTING WORDS.

DO YOU HAVE A FAMILY?

DO I HAVE A **WHAT**??

INCREDULOUS ED

ED, DO YOU HAVE THE LATEST BUDGET NUMBERS?

BUDGET??? WHAT IS A "BUDGET"? AND WHY IN THE WORLD WOULD I HAVE ONE?

BECAUSE YOU'RE THE BUDGET MANAGER.

HERE YOU GO.

I FOUND THE ULTIMATE TOOL FOR THE MOBILE PROFESSIONAL.

IT'S A COMBINATION PDA, PHONE, PAGER, DIGITAL CAMERA, FAX, E-MAIL, LAPTOP AND SHREDDER.

IT CLIPS RIGHT TO MY BELT!

CAROL, ORDER AN EXTRA BATTERY FOR MY MOBILE TECHNOLOGY PLATFORM.

DO YOU WANT THE ONE THAT STRAPS TO YOUR BACK OR THE ONE WITH ITS OWN WHEELBARROW?

I THINK I JUST LOST A LUNG.

I CAN'T GIVE YOU A RAISE BECAUSE YOU DON'T ASK ENOUGH QUESTIONS IN MEETINGS.

QUESTIONS SHOW THAT YOU CARE ABOUT YOUR JOB AND HAVE A THIRST FOR KNOWLEDGE.

WHO ELSE LIKES WOOD?

WE SHOULD READ THE SET-UP INSTRUCTIONS.

ALICE, A TRUE ENGINEER NEVER READS THE SET-UP INSTRUCTIONS.

IT SAYS TO KEEP IT AWAY FROM ANY SLURPING SOUNDS.

GAAA!!

WHAT'S THE LOWEST RATIO OF WORK-TO-GABBING THAT IS STILL CONSIDERED "WORK"?

I'D HAVE TO SAY ONE-IN-EIGHT, MAYBE ONE-IN-NINE.

SOUNDS RIGHT.

DOES TALKING ABOUT WORK COUNT AS WORK?

WELL...I'M NOT ENJOYING IT.

WE'RE CUTTING BACK ON ADVERTISING TO BOOST EARNINGS.

UM...EXCUSE ME. I'LL BE RIGHT BACK.

ME TOO.

WE GOT ANOTHER MASS EXODUS DOORWAY JAM.

THIS WILL BE YOUR NEW MOTTO...

DANCE LIKE IT HURTS. LOVE LIKE YOU NEED MONEY. WORK WHEN PEOPLE ARE WATCHING.

YOU CAN'T ASSIGN MOTTOS TO ME.

YOU'D BETTER READ OUR CONTRACT.

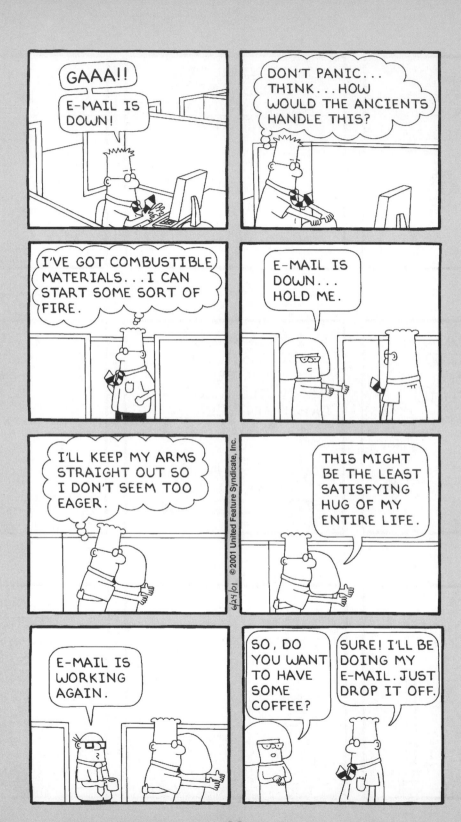

PER MARKETING'S REQUEST, I DID AN O.R.D. FOR THE B.G.G. THAT RESULTED IN A Q.R.B.

THEN I DISCOVERED THAT MARKETING USES THOSE ACRONYMS FOR DIFFERENT THINGS.

THEIR VERSION DOESN'T REQUIRE NUDITY, JUST TO PICK ONE EXAMPLE.

I'VE DECIDED TO BECOME A PERFECTIONIST.

THAT WAY I'LL HAVE MORE REASONS TO HATE PEOPLE.

YOUR ROCK IS ERODING WRONG.

WE'RE HAVING A MEETING TO DISCUSS EMPLOYEE RETENTION.

TELL THEM THAT EMPLOYEES QUIT BECAUSE THERE ARE TOO MANY USELESS MEETINGS.

WE WON'T BE GETTING INTO REASONS AT THE FIRST MEETING.

YOU'RE UNDER-STAFFED AND OVERWORKED.

SO I HIRED A STRESS COUNSELOR AND ANOTHER MANAGER TO GLARE AT YOU.

RELAX... DEEP BREATHS... THERE...

FROM NOW ON I'LL BE MANAGING BY EXCEPTION.

IF I DON'T TALK TO YOU FOR MONTHS, ASSUME YOU'RE DOING A GOOD JOB.

...OR THAT YOUR PROJECT ISN'T IMPORTANT...OR I DON'T REMEMBER YOUR NAME.

IT NEEDS TO BE SO EASY THAT YOUR MOTHER COULD USE IT.

MY MOTHER ISN'T A MORON. MAYBE WE COULD USE YOUR MOTHER AS THE TEST.

WHAT MAKES YOU THINK MY MOTHER IS A MORON?

SHE FED YOU.

FRANKLY, THE JOB IS A REAL NO-BRAINER.

YOUR RÉSUMÉ IS A BLANK PIECE OF PAPER; I LIKE A MAN WHO CAN BE BRIEF.

YOU'RE RUINING MY DONUT EXPERIENCE.

I HEARD A RUMOR THAT THERE MIGHT BE LAYOFFS ON FRIDAY. IS IT TRUE?

ABSOLUTELY NOT. NO WAY. NOPE. NEGATORY. NO, NO, NO, NO, NO.

GREAT. CAN I TAKE OFF FRIDAY?

MONDAY WOULD BE BETTER.

LAYOFF PLANNING

LET'S FIRE ALL THE PEOPLE WHO GIVE US THE CREEPS...

...ALL THE PEOPLE WITH EXCESSIVE NOSE HAIR AND ANYONE WHO INSISTS ON BEING CALLED "DOCTOR."

YOU'VE GOT A FIVE-MINUTE MEETING ON FRIDAY, DOCTOR WOLFINGTON.

 MONTY, YOU'RE NOT GROWING INTO YOUR JOB AS QUICKLY AS I HOPED.

 SO I SIGNED YOU UP FOR AN ACCELERATED EVOLUTION PROGRAM. THEY PACK A MILLION YEARS INTO A TWO-DAY CLASS.

 HURRY UP! WE'VE ALREADY LOST THE OPPOSABLE THUMBS MODULE; LET'S NOT LOSE FIRE TOO.

 EVOLUTION TRAINING

SOME OF YOU WILL NOT MAKE IT THROUGH THE CLASS.

 MAY I MOVE TO A DIFFERENT SEAT?

 SURE...OOPS. PROBLEM SOLVED.

CARL, DON'T LEAVE THAT WHERE SOMEONE WILL SLIP ON IT.

 EVOLUTION TRAINING

ZOLTAR IS A GRADUATE OF THIS CLASS. HE WILL DEMONSTRATE SPEED EVOLVING.

 UNH...ERRR... HOO...AHH...

 I HOPE YOU'RE STARING AT MY NEW SIDEBURNS.

BY THE END OF MY TWO-DAY EVOLUTION CLASS I HAD ONE SURVIVING STUDENT.

HE'S PROBABLY THE COCKIEST SQUIRREL I'VE EVER SEEN. TOWARD THE END HE WEIGHED THREE THOUSAND POUNDS.

IF YOU ASKED ME WHO'S THE UNLUCK-IEST PERSON IN THE WORLD, I'D HAVE TO SAY IT WAS THE JANITOR.

THE COMPANY DID WELL SO YOU GET A BONUS DESPITE THE FACT YOU DID NO WORK ALL YEAR.

I'D FIRE YOU BUT I CAN'T REPLACE YOU BECAUSE THERE'S A HIRING FREEZE AND I DON'T WANT TO SHRINK MY EMPIRE.

THIS MIGHT BE A HAND-SHAKING SITUATION BUT I DON'T KNOW WHERE YOUR HAND HAS BEEN.

OFF YOU GO.

I'VE BEEN TRAPPED IN MY OFFICE FOR THREE DAYS! DIDN'T YOU HEAR ME SCREAM?

I USED MY STAPLE REMOVER TO CLAW THROUGH THE SIDE WALL!

YOUR DOOR IS A PULL, NOT A PUSH.

GET ME A BIGGER STAPLE REMOVER JUST TO BE SAFE.

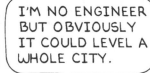

HOW CAN YOU WRITE REVIEWS OF MOVIES YOU HAVEN'T SEEN?

EASILY.

"THROW AWAY YOUR PICASSO PAINTINGS. 'NIGHT OF THE LIVING SQUIRREL' IS THE ONLY ART YOU'LL EVER NEED."

HOW MUCH IS THE STUDIO PAYING YOU?

DANG... TOO OBVIOUS.

HELLO...YES, I'D LIKE TO BUY A RAVE REVIEW FOR MY NEW MOVIE.

CAN YOU AFFORD "SUSPENSEFUL THRILL RIDE" OR WOULD YOU LIKE SOMETHING MORE IN THE "DELIGHT-FUL" PRICE RANGE.

I'M RELEASING IT ON NEW YEAR'S DAY; CAN YOU GIVE ME A PRICE FOR "BEST COMEDY SO FAR THIS YEAR"?

THE CLEAN DESK AWARD GOES TO WALLY.

MAYBE WALLY CAN SHARE SOME TIPS ON KEEPING OUR DESKS CLUTTER-FREE.

I USUALLY THROW AWAY THIS SORT OF THING IN THE MEN'S ROOM ON THE WAY BACK TO MY CUBICLE.

INTRODUCING "MORALE MONEY." NOW YOU CAN EARN PLAY MONEY FOR DOING GOOD WORK.

YOU CAN USE IT AT THE COMPANY STORE TO BUY PRODUCTS THAT HAVE OUR LOGO.

THE COFFEE MUG COSTS TEN MILLION MORALE DOLLARS.

MAY I HAVE AN ERGONOMIC EVALUATION OF MY CHAIR AND KEYBOARD?

ASOK, WORK IS SUPPOSED TO HURT. THAT'S HOW YOU KNOW YOU'RE DOING IT RIGHT.

I CAN'T FEEL MY HANDS!

MY WHOLE BODY IS NUMB!

THE CURE FOR CARPAL TUNNEL IS TO EAT SIX BANANAS A DAY.

THAT'S WHAT I DO AND I HAVE THE HANDS OF A TEENAGER.

DO YOU HAVE ANY DATA TO SUPPORT YOUR MEDICAL ADVICE?

DOES A HUGE PIMPLE COUNT?

BOB WAS WORKING FOR YOU WHEN HE DIED. THE FAMILY WANTS YOU TO SAY SOMETHING AT HIS FUNERAL.

I BARELY KNEW HIM. MAYBE I CAN READ SOMETHING FROM HIS LAST PERFORMANCE REVIEW.

BOB NEEDS TO WORK ON HIS COMMUNICATION SKILLS ... AND ATTENDANCE.

CUSTOMER SERVICE

FIND THE SERIAL NUMBER BY PULVERIZING THE CASE WITH A HAMMER.

ARE YOU SURE THIS WON'T VOID MY WARRANTY?

IT'S NOT ALWAYS ABOUT YOU.

I CAN ANALYZE YOUR EMPLOYEES' HANDWRITING TO FIND OUT WHO MIGHT STEAL.

HAS HANDWRITING ANALYSIS BEEN TESTED IN DOUBLE-BLIND SCIENTIFIC STUDIES?

YES, BUT THE SCIENTISTS DOTTED THEIR I's WITH SMILEY FACES SO I KNOW THEY'RE LIARS.

WOW!

HANDWRITING ANALYSIS

YOUR HANDWRITING PROVES THAT YOU'RE A DISTURBED LONER WHO STEALS.

WHAT?

TAKE THIS THIEF AWAY!

IS THIS PART ABSOLUTELY NECESSARY?

LIBERAL

CATBERT: EVIL H.R. DIRECTOR

THE AVERAGE PERFORMANCE EVALUATION FOR YOUR GROUP IS TOO HIGH.

DO YOU WANT ME TO LOWER THEIR RATINGS OR THEIR ACTUAL PERFORMANCE?

WHATEVER

THIS IS STARTING TO AFFECT MY PERFORMANCE.

WHY? I'M NOT TOUCHING YOU.

MY POWERS OF COMMUNICATION WILL INSPIRE THEM TO BE BETTER EMPLOYEES.

GAAA!! HE'S USING HIS POWERS OF COMMUNICATION AGAINST US!

MUST WORK HARDER FOR NO GOOD REASON.

WE'RE TOO LATE!

EACH OF US MUST DO HIS PART TO SAVE ENERGY.

ZZZZZ

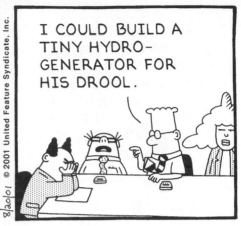

I COULD BUILD A TINY HYDRO-GENERATOR FOR HIS DROOL.

I'M TIRED OF DATING ATTRACTIVE MEN WHO ARE DUMB AND SELF-CENTERED.

MAYBE I CAN FIND AN INTELLIGENT HOMELY GUY AND CLEAN HIM UP.

NO!!!

DO YOU MIND IF I WORK IN A SET WITH THOSE FIVE-POUNDERS?

DON'T DO IT, AMBER!

I MADE A LIST OF ALL THE WAYS YOU NEED TO IMPROVE IN ORDER TO KEEP DATING ME.

LOSE FORTY POUNDS, NEW WARDROBE, NEW HAIRCUT, NEW CAR, NEW ODOR...

BUT YOUR DOG IS PERFECT. HOW'D THAT HAPPEN?

WHEN CAN YOU MOVE IN?

95

MY PERFORMANCE EXCEEDS EXPECTATIONS BUT MY PAY IS BASED ON MARKET AVERAGES.

I FIGURE SOME UNDERACHIEVERS ARE GETTING THE EXTRA MONEY THAT I EARN.

GIVE ME THEIR NAMES SO I CAN GO GET MY MONEY.

IT'S WALLY.

FIRST, WE'LL LOWER COSTS BY OFFERING A RETIREMENT PACKAGE THAT INDUCES ALL THE SMART EMPLOYEES TO LEAVE.

THEN WE'LL REWRITE OUR MISSION STATEMENT TO MAKE IT FIT BETTER.

OUR NEW MISSION STATEMENT IS, "IF YOU CAN READ THIS YOU SHOULD HAVE RETIRED BY NOW."

OUCH

I'VE AGREED TO BE IN THE DUNKING TANK FOR THIS YEAR'S UNITED CHARITY DAY.

BONK!!

I DON'T LIKE LINES.

MY KEYBOARD IS BROKEN. IT ONLY TYPES ASTERISKS FOR PASSWORDS.

DOGBERT'S TECH SUPPORT

TRY CHANGING YOUR PASSWORD TO FIVE ASTERISKS.

I HOPE I CAN REMEMBER IT.

IS THERE MORE TO LIFE THAN JUST WORKING?

YES, THERE'S ALSO THE COMPLAINING ABOUT WORK, THE NIGHTLY PERIODS OF UNCONSCIOUSNESS AND SWEET, SWEET DEATH.

MAYBE I SHOULD HAVE KIDS.

TO SHARE THE JOY?

ALICE, YOU HAVE TO LEARN HOW TO TAKE RISKS.

YOU MEAN LIKE QUITTING THIS PUTRID COMPANY AND GOING TO WORK SOMEPLACE BETTER?

WHY DOESN'T ANYONE UNDERSTAND ANYTHING I SAY?

THREE O'CLOCK.

ALL OF OUR DATA IS GROSSLY INACCURATE... BUT I NEED DATA IN ORDER TO MANAGE.

IF I CONCENTRATE HARD ENOUGH I CAN FORGET THAT THE DATA IS BAD, THEN I CAN USE IT.

I HAVE TO GIVE HIM CREDIT; MANAGING IS HARDER THAN IT LOOKS.

I'M BEING MOVED TO THE MAGIC PORTAL, CUBICLE 4S750R!

EVERYONE WHO SITS IN THE MAGIC PORTAL GETS A BETTER JOB WITHIN SIX MONTHS!

THERE ISN'T A CUBICLE 4S750R, IS THERE?

THE FIRST ROUND OF LAYOFFS ARE ALWAYS THE CRUELEST.

ED, I WANT YOU TO CROSSTRAIN ASOK ON THE ACCOUNTING SYSTEM.

AND DON'T WORRY THAT YOU'LL LOSE RESPECT AND JOB SECURITY IF ASOK LEARNS YOUR WHOLE JOB IN ONE DAY.

I DON'T THINK "ACCOUNTS RECEIVABLE" IS AN EXPENSE.

NO ONE HAS COMPLAINED YET.

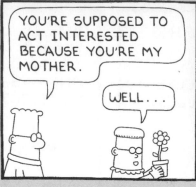

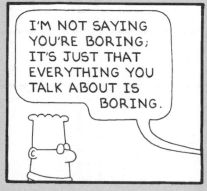

© 2001 United Feature Syndicate, Inc.

COULD YOU TURN OFF THE MUSIC? I CAN'T CONCENTRATE.

HOW ABOUT IF I TURN IT DOWN TO A LEVEL WHERE IT STILL DRIVES YOU NUTS BUT YOU'RE TOO SHY TO COMPLAIN A SECOND TIME?

THANK YOU.

IT MIGHT CREEP UP OVER TIME.

ASOK, YOU'RE COMING WITH ME TO AN IMPORTANT MEETING ACROSS THE BRIDGE.

IMPORTANT!

MY HARD WORK AS AN INTERN IS PAYING OFF. ALREADY I AM INVITED TO AN IMPORTANT MEETING!

HEY, WE GET THE CARPOOL LANE!

WHAT DO YOU GUYS THINK ABOUT MY NEW HAIRCUT?

IT'S A GARGANTUAN MISTAKE THAT WILL RUIN YOUR LIFE, FRIGHTEN CHILDREN AND BRUISE FRUIT.

I'M ALL FROZE UP! NO ONE EVER ASKED FOR MY OPINION BEFORE!

LOOK, I HAVE THREE COMPUTERS IN THE HOUSE. ALL THREE SIMULTANEOUSLY LOST E-MAIL BUT NOT WEB FUNCTION.

THAT MEANS THE PROBLEM IS IN YOUR E-MAIL SERVICE. CAN YOU GRASP THAT CONCEPT?

OKAY, I'M RE-ENTERING MY ACCOUNT INFORMATION... HEY, GUESS WHAT? THAT DIDN'T WORK EITHER.

I NEED A BRILLIANT EMPLOYEE TO BE MY ASSISTANT MANAGER.

THAT'S WHY I CAME TO YOU.

THAT'S THE FIRST NICE THING...

YOUR JOB IS TO CLONE ME.

OUR POINTY-HAIRED BOSS ASKED ME TO CLONE HIM.

WHAT IF HIS CLONE HAS NO SOUL?

IF?

IF?

YES, THE TECHNOLOGY TO CLONE YOU EXISTS, BUT IT'S ILLEGAL TO CLONE HUMANS.

IF THE COPS FIND OUT, WE CAN FRAME MY CLONE FOR THE CRIME.

THAT IS SO WRONG.

WHY? HE'D DO THE SAME THING TO ME!

MY BOSS ASKED ME TO CLONE HIM. IS THAT ETHICAL?

YOU'LL EITHER CREATE A SOULLESS ABOMINATION OR, IF THE CLONE IS NORMAL, YOU WILL HAVE SHOWN THAT SOULS ARE IRRELEVANT.

WHAT IF THE ORIGINAL IS ALREADY A SOULLESS ABOMINATION?

YOU CAN BORROW MY CLONER. IT'S IN THE TRUCK.

CLONING THE BOSS

WILL THIS HURT?

I HOPE SO.

WE HEARD IT MIGHT HURT.

MAY I PUSH THE BUTTON?

CLONING THE BOSS

THERE'S A PROBLEM WITH YOUR CLONE.

WALLY SPILLED SODA ON THE DNA MODULE. YOUR CLONE IS ONE-HALF HORSE POSTERIOR.

AND ONE-HALF THAT ISN'T LIKE YOU.

I'M A CLONE OF YOUR BOSS?

THE PROCEDURE DIDN'T EXACTLY WORK. SO YOU'RE NOT SO MUCH A HUMAN BEING AS YOU ARE A...

GOD?

KNICKKNACK.

YOU'VE GOT TO IMPLEMENT A SIX SIGMA PROGRAM OR ELSE YOU'RE DOOMED.

AREN'T YOU THE SAME CONSULTANT WHO SOLD US THE WORTHLESS TQM PROGRAM A FEW YEARS AGO?

I ASSURE YOU THAT THIS PROGRAM HAS A TOTALLY, TOTALLY DIFFERENT NAME.

WHEN CAN WE START?

SIX SIGMA CONSULTANT

EVERY COMPANY THAT USED MY SIX SIGMA PROGRAM INCREASED PROFITS.

...EXCEPT FOR THE ONES THAT WERE IN INDUSTRY DOWNTURNS...

...OR FLAT GROWTH INDUSTRIES...OR INDUSTRIES THAT ONLY UPTURNED A LITTLE BIT.

SIX SIGMA CONSULTANT

ALL OF YOU ARE SELFISH AND DIMWITTED BUT DON'T WORRY.

I'LL TEACH YOU A PROCESS THAT WILL BOG YOU DOWN IN MEETINGS SO YOU CAN'T HURT ANYTHING.

I CAN'T MOVE MY ARMS!

ZZZ ZZZ ZZZ ZZZZ

SIX SIGMA CONSULTANT

THE FIRST STEP IS TO IDENTIFY YOUR PROBLEMS.

WE DON'T HAVE ANY PROBLEMS. WHAT'S THE SECOND STEP?

MUST... CONTROL ...FIST.

I HOPE SOMEONE GIVES ME A BELT.

HAPPY SERVICE ANNIVERSARY, ALICE.

WE'RE OUT OF TWENTY-YEAR PINS SO I GOT TWENTY OF THE ONE-YEAR PINS.

YOU CAN PIN THESE BABIES ALL OVER YOUR BLOUSE...OR FISHING HAT IF YOU PREFER.

THE CARD SAYS, "TO KATHY" BUT IT WAS NEVER OPENED. FOR SOME REASON SHE QUIT THE DAY SHE GOT HER TWENTY PINS.

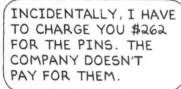

INCIDENTALLY, I HAVE TO CHARGE YOU $262 FOR THE PINS. THE COMPANY DOESN'T PAY FOR THEM.

FIRST OF ALL, I'VE ONLY WORKED HERE FOR ABOUT SIX YEARS...

WOW. YOU LOOK OLDER.

ANYWAY, JUST GIVE ME THE $262 AND THROW AWAY EIGHT PINS AND WE'LL CALL IT GOOD.

WHY ARE YOU ROLLING UP YOUR SLEEVE? ARE YOU GOING TO PIN THEM TO YOUR ARM?

Panel 1: CARL, YOU'RE ONLY A CONTRACTOR. YOU HAVE TO STOP USING COMPANY RESOURCES.

Panel 2: MMN NPH HBM MRM!

YES, I KNOW YOU BRING YOUR OWN AIR, BUT YOU STILL USE OUR GRAVITY.

Panel 3: FBM GMP RKR!

IF IT'S NOT TOO MUCH TO ASK, COULD YOU HOVER?

Panel 4: ANNE L. RETENTIVE

ANNE, I'M GOING TO TASK YOU WITH A DELIVERABLE.

Panel 5: GAAA!! TASK IS NOT A VERB!! MY WORLD IS FALLING APART!

Panel 6: TOMORROW I'LL ASK HER TO TIMELINE HER PROJECT.

Panel 7: I HAVE DISCOVERED THE CAUSE OF OUR NETWORK OUTAGES.

LAN

Panel 8: SOME IDIOT IS USING OUR NETWORK ROOM FOR MEETINGS AND UNPLUGGING THE SERVER BECAUSE IT'S TOO NOISY.

Panel 9: A SERVER IS LIKE A WAITRESS, RIGHT?

YEAH, A NOISY ONE.

I'D BE A GOOD STOCK MARKET EXPERT.

I'D BUY STOCKS AND THEN GO ON TV AND RECOMMEND THEM SO THEY GO UP.

WHAT ABOUT THE FUNDAMENTALS?

IT DOESN'T GET MORE FUNDAMENTAL THAN THAT!

STOCK MARKET EXPERT

CLIP THIS MICRO-PHONE TO YOUR FUR. WE'RE LIVE IN TWO.

MAKE SURE MY TAIL IS OFF CAMERA. I'LL BE RECOMMENDING STOCKS I OWN AND THAT SORT OF THING MAKES ME WAG.

SOMEDAY I GOTTA GET HONEST WORK.

STOCK MARKET EXPERT

...EVERYONE SHOULD BUY STOCK IN THAT COMPANY. SELL YOUR HOUSE IF NECESSARY.

SHOULD WE WORRY THAT THE P/E IS 900, YOUR TRACK RECORD IS TERRIBLE AND YOU ONLY RECOMMEND STOCKS YOU OWN?

WELL, RON, AS YOU CAN SEE FROM THE ONE-WEEK CHART, THIS STOCK ONLY GOES UP.

BUY! BUY!

STOCK MARKET EXPERT

IF YOUR CORE HOLDING IS A FALLING KNIFE, YOU CAN DOLLAR COST AVERAGE THROUGH THE DEAD CAT BOUNCE.

MY SECRET ECONOMIC MODEL SAYS YOU SHOULD CHANGE YOUR CASH ALLOCATION FROM 12.4% TO 12.3%.

MY NEW BOOK IS, "IF YOU AREN'T CHURNING, YOU AREN'T LEARNING."

DON'T COME BACK.

WE NEED TO HAVE AN ALL-COMPANY MEETING TO TALK ABOUT THE LAYOFFS.

YOU MIGHT GET SOME HOSTILE QUESTIONS OWING TO THE FACT THAT THEY FOUND OUT ABOUT THE LAY-OFFS BY READING THE NEWSPAPER.

NO, I'VE NEVER NOTICED THAT I LEAVE A TRAIL OF REEKING SLIME WHEREVER I SLITHER.

I'LL TAKE ONE MORE QUESTION ABOUT THE LAYOFFS... YES, YOU IN THE BACK.

AND I'D APPRECIATE IT IF THIS QUESTION DIDN'T INVOLVE MY ODOR, MY DNA, OR ANY COMPARISONS TO RODENTS, SNAKES OR WEASELS.

NEVER MIND.

MY HOME PHONE TURNS INTO A TALKING CLOCK AFTER MIDNIGHT.

YEAH, I DIDN'T BELIEVE IT EITHER UNTIL WALLY TAUGHT ME HOW TO USE IT.

IT'S 3:14 IN THE MORNING YOU #%⌢!* IDIOT!

YUP

THEN I NOTICED THAT THE CIRCUIT DESIGN LOOKED LIKE A BUG. I WAS GOING TO MENTION IT BUT THEN I DIDN'T.

I'M PSYCHIC!

UNLESS YOU'RE SAYING OUT LOUD EVERY THOUGHT THAT CROSSES YOUR MIND.

IT'S CALLED CONVER-SATION.

ASOK, I WANT YOU TO WORK FOR THE EVIL DIRECTOR OF HUMAN RESOURCES UNTIL HIS ASSISTANT RECOVERS.

FROM WHAT IS HE RECOVERING? IS IT A COLD OR PERHAPS A FLU?

HE SAW SO MUCH EVIL THAT HIS SOUL DISSOLVED AND HE BECAME A WINGED DEMON.

CATBERT: EVIL H.R. DIRECTOR

WE'RE ALMOST OUT OF KITTY LITTER.

GATHER ALL THE RÉSUMÉS WE GOT THIS WEEK AND RUN THEM THROUGH THE SHREDDER.

SHOULDN'T WE BE MATCHING THESE WITH OUR OPENINGS?

THAT'S WHAT WE'RE DOING.

ASOK WORKS IN H.R.

ASOK, I WANT YOU TO HANDLE ALL THE HARASSMENT COMPLAINTS.

AND AS I LEFT THE ROOM I COULD FEEL ALICE'S EYES CHECKING OUT MY CABOOSE.

SO...YOU HAVE PSYCHIC POWERS?

MY EYES ARE UP HERE, PAL.

ASOK WORKS IN H.R.

IF WE ELIMINATE VACATION DAYS AND INCREASE SICK DAYS...

WOULD THE EMPLOYEES FALL FOR OUR TRAP AND MAKE THEMSELVES SICK TO GET DAYS OFF?

WHAT?!!

YOU'RE IN H.R. NOW. IT'S OKAY TO BE EVIL.

EVIL, RIGHT.

© 2001 United Feature Syndicate, Inc.